MW01131650

Exploring for Shipwrecks

KC Smith

Franklin Watts
A Division of Grolier Publishing
New York • London • Hong Kong • Sydney
Danbury, Connecticut

*To Rudy, who immediately learned about the fascination and excitement
of shipwrecks and seafaring from his humans*

Note to readers: Definitions for words in **bold** can be found in the Glossary at the back
of this book.

Photographs ©: Archive Photos: 29 (Bob Padgett/Reuters), 3 top, 26; Brian Skerry: 3 bottom, 38, 39, 43;
Christie's Images: 23 (Thomas Luny); Corbis-Bettmann: 30 (Jonathan Blair), 42 (Amos Nachoum), 44 (Jim
Sugar); INA: 15, 27, 33, 40, 48, 52 (KC Smith), 8 (KC Smith/Cayman Island Project), 12 (KC
Smith/Columbus Caravels Project); Liaison Agency, Inc.: 47 (Michael Justice), 14, 17, 18, 19 (Nicolas Le
Corre), 45 (C. Rives), 51 (Eric Brissaud); National Geographic Image Collection: 7 (Sisse Brimberg), 16
(Bates Littlehales); Photo Researchers: 25 (Noble Proctor); Stock Boston: 20, 21 (Mike Mazzaschi);
Superstock, Inc.: 36; The Image Works: 35 (Mark Godfrey); Tom Stack & Associates: 10 (Brian Parker);
Tony Stone Images: 4 (Chris Simpson).

Cover illustration by Greg Harris.

Visit Franklin Watts on the Internet at: http://publishing.grolier.com

Library of Congress Cataloging-in-Publication Data

Smith, KC
    Exploring for shipwrecks / KC Smith.
        p.   cm.— (Watts Library)
    Includes bibliographical references and index.
    Summary: Introduces the discipline of underwater archaeology and the techniques used to find and
study submerged ships.
    ISBN: 0-531-20377-8 (lib. bdg.)   0-531-16471-3 (pbk.)
    1. Underwater archaeology Juvenile literature. 2. Shipwrecks Juvenile literature. 3. Excavations
(Archaeology) Juvenile literature. [1. Shipwrecks. 2. Underwater archaeology.] I. Title. II. Series.
CC77.U5S57 2000
930.1'028'04—dc21   99-40537
                                                        CIP

© 2000 Franklin Watts, a division of Grolier Publishing
All rights reserved. Published simultaneously in Canada.
Printed in the United States of America.
1 2 3 4 5 6 7 8 9 10 R 09 08 07 06 05 04 03 02 01 00

Contents

Chapter One
A Shipwreck Experience 5

Chapter Two
Knowing Before Going 11

Chapter Three
A Unique Time Capsule 21

Chapter Four
Secrets to Success 31

Chapter Five
Tools of the Trade 39

Chapter Six
More Than a Pile of Rocks 49

Chapter Seven
Exploring On Your Own 52

54 **Glossary**

57 **To Find Out More**

60 **A Note on Sources**

61 **Index**

A diver explores the underwater world.

A Shipwreck Experience

The only sound I heard was the rush of air bubbles escaping from my mouthpiece every time I exhaled. The bubbles bounced along the sides of my face as they floated to the surface 15 feet (4.6 meters) above me.

I was swimming slowly above the seabed, propelled by the long black fins that I had strapped to my feet before jumping off the boat. The water was warm and clear; it seemed as though I could see for miles. Around me, brightly colored fish darted here and there, sea plants waved in the current, and crabs popped into their holes. It would have been easy to stop and watch for hours, but I was on a mission, looking for something important.

With an extra kick of my fins, I swam up and over some coralheads. Oddly shaped and beautifully colored, coralheads are formed by colonies of microscopic animals that live in warm, shallow water. Dense patches of their rocklike dwellings are called reefs. Countless sea creatures find food and shelter in the nooks and crannies of a coral reef.

As lovely as they are, reefs can be dangerous. Their rough surfaces will cut a careless scuba diver or the bottom of a ship. Many vessels have sunk after crashing on a reef during a storm or because of an error in navigation.

Sometime in the past, a ship sank on a reef in the bay where I was diving. Local fishers had told the members of our archaeological team about the shipwreck. When they hauled in their nets, they sometimes found old objects mixed in with their catch. After they showed us the location on a navigational chart of the bay, it didn't take us long to find the site.

On our very first dive, we found a clue—a pile of round rocks that had come from dry land. Disguised by sea plants, shells, and a crust of coral, this mound was no mystery to us. It was the **ballast** stones that the ship carried in its **hull** to remain stable in the water. As we continued to explore, we discovered bits of pottery and glass trapped in holes around the

coralheads. When we fanned away the sand with our hands, we found pieces of wood that had been shaped with a saw.

But these **artifacts** were not enough to tell us where the ship came from, when it sailed, or why it sank. While other members of the team measured and mapped the remains, I searched the surrounding area, looking for additional clues.

And then I saw it! It looked like a crusty white doughnut, partially hidden by shells and dead coral that cover the seabed like leaves on a sidewalk in the fall. But this was different!

Lead weights or cannonballs from a wreck in the 1600s

7

These olive jars are from the project that author KC Smith worked on.

Nature doesn't make shapes that are perfectly round or straight. **Archaeologists** know this fact, which helps them recognize human-made objects on land and underwater. Before I put the new evidence into my artifact bag, I placed a bright plastic flag into the seabed so I could find the location again.

At the end of the day, the team members examined the object. We knew from past experience that it was the mouth, or rim, of a pottery jug called an olive jar. Hundreds of years ago, Europeans shipped foods and liquids in large clay pots sealed with corks. Over time, the size and shape of the jars changed. Archaeologists have a good idea about when these changes took place. Olive jars with rims like the one that I recovered were used by Spaniards in the middle of the 1600s. My unexpected find was a very good clue.

For several days, we studied this wreck in the Cayman Islands and uncovered additional evidence of its seventeenth-century Spanish origin. Later, the project director searched for historic documents to explain the vessel's sinking. He located records in Jamaica and Spain that described an attack by Spanish privateers on an English fishing station on Little Cayman in 1670. The wreck that we had studied was a casualty of that encounter.

Do you think that you would recognize an underwater wreck if you found one?

Chapter Two

Knowing Before Going

If you wanted to find a shipwreck, where would you look? Would you search only in the ocean? What tools would you use? How would you recognize a wreck if you found one?

Anyone can put on a mask and fins and go exploring for a shipwreck, but the chances of actually finding one are slim. Underwater archaeologists earn their living by locating, examining, and explaining shipwrecks and other under-water remains. They study wrecks to

Who Does What?

Archaeologists study past human cultures. Paleontologists study dinosaurs and other fossil remains.

Cataloging information after excavation is an important part of any shipwreck project. This researcher logs in a collection of pipes.

understand how people built and used ships in the past and how watercraft have affected human **cultures**.

But how do they know where to look? What do they do when they find a wreck? To understand how these professionals work, you need to know a little bit about archaeology.

The Science of People

Archaeology is the study of past cultures based on artifacts and other evidence. Archaeologists work on land and underwater to recover remains that they use to describe how groups of people were organized, how they survived, what tools and technologies they used, and what their beliefs were. Archaeologists also explain how people adapted to or were changed by different natural environments.

When researchers study an archaeological site—a place where human activity occurred, they employ the **scientific method**. They develop a **hypothesis** about what they will learn and specific questions they want to answer. They make a plan for testing the hypothesis and gathering evidence to answer the questions. The hypothesis may change as information is collected, and new questions always arise. When the project is over, they write a report about their findings and conclusions. They also ensure that artifacts are treated properly so that they will survive in the future. All archaeologists use the same basic methods and scientific principles, but those who work underwater need different tools because the environment is different from that on land.

Watery Work

Underwater archaeologists study sites that are submerged in the freshwater of lakes or rivers or the salt water of harbors and oceans. Most study historic ships and boats that have wrecked or have been abandoned, but they also explore ports and cities, prehistoric villages and camps, and other remains that have become submerged.

People have explored shipwrecks and other watery sites for thousands of years, but underwater archaeology as a recognized field is relatively new. As the discipline has grown, it has become more specialized. Today, people who do this work usually become experts in a particular culture, time period, or type of site.

Prehistoric underwater archaeologists learn about human activity around water that occurred before written records were kept. **Maritime archaeologists** are interested in seafaring—travel by sea—in the broadest sense. They examine the ships, people, and societies that were involved in seafaring.

The First Project

The first scientific shipwreck study was conducted in the early 1960s at Cape Gelidonya in Turkey. The vessel was about 3,000 years old.

13

Conservators work to protect the remains of a shipwreck.

Nautical archaeologists focus on watercraft, including ships, boats, canoes, rafts, and other forms of floating transportation. They study how and why vessels were built, what kind of equipment and skills were needed to operate them, and what routes were traveled.

You don't have to get wet to be involved in underwater research. For example, some archaeologists concentrate on the treatment of remains after they have been recovered. This process restores objects and ensures that they will survive when they are dry; it is called **conservation**.

An artist sketching an artifact

Because archaeological sites are very complex, research projects need a team of people who have different knowledge and skills. A shipwreck project typically includes a director, a fieldwork supervisor, a diving officer, a **conservator**, a mechanic, a photographer, a videographer, an artist, and divers, who may be students or volunteers. Although each person has an assignment, team members usually can carry out many of the tasks. In addition, the director consults experts outside the team when a unique artifact is found or a special test is needed.

Important Training

People who want to become underwater archaeologists go to college to study archaeology, anthropology, history, geography, science, art, and other related subjects. To learn the techniques for examining and explaining sites, they work on a shipwreck project or attend a field school conducted by professionals. Individuals who wish to teach students or direct a shipwreck excavation continue in school until they have earned a master's or doctorate degree. In this photo, students practice underwater archaeological methods on a plastic model in a swimming pool.

Scientists and Scoundrels

Underwater archaeologists are trained professionals who study submerged cultural sites scientifically, conserve the artifacts, and publish their findings. These practices distinguish them from **treasure hunters**, who also work on shipwrecks.

Treasure hunters do not use standard methods of **excavation** and sometimes ignore or destroy important evidence. Because their only interest is financial, treasure hunters sell artifacts or use them to repay investors. They often neglect artifact conservation and rarely write about their discoveries.

Archaeologists do not keep, buy, sell, or trade any artifacts. They believe that cultural sites belong to the public and that recovered objects should be kept together for study or display in a museum for everyone to see.

If they don't get to keep the artifacts, why do underwater archaeologists work on shipwrecks? Why would anyone be interested in a pile of rocks, broken bits of pottery and glass, and pieces of waterlogged wood?

Underwater archaeologists piece together artifacts and other evidence to learn about past cultures.

For underwater archaeologists, submerged sites are like great big puzzles. The challenge is to fit the pieces together and create a picture of the past. Because wrecks are usually jumbled and some evidence does not survive, it isn't easy. Archaeologists are fascinated by history and past cultures, and they want to discover details that were previously unknown.

Saving the Past for the Future

Archaeologists strive to protect cultural sites on land and underwater so that information about the past will be available in the future. Unfortunately, archaeological sites are subjected to many destructive forces, including weather, development, vandalism, looting, and treasure hunting.

Researchers examine and record underwater remains to determine how important, fragile, or threatened they are. With this information, they make plans and laws designed to protect and preserve the past. When a site must be destroyed because it lies in the path of new construction, archaeologists try to recover as much evidence as possible before the information is lost forever.

Careful documentation of a wreck site helps preserve maritime history.

These grounded schooners may one day serve as unique time capsules.

Chapter Three

A Unique Time Capsule

People have used watercraft for thousands of years to explore, transport themselves and their goods, go into battle, spread ideas, establish colonies, and travel for pleasure. The earliest vessels were rafts made of bundled reeds or logs tied together and boats made of animal skins stretched over a frame of branches. They carried one or two people and a few supplies as they floated along quiet waterways. Today, aircraft carriers and supertankers with metal hulls cross the world's oceans carrying thousands of tons of cargo and thousands of crew members.

But consider this. Throughout history, each vessel that made a successful trip left few clues about its voyage. It went out, conducted its business, and returned. Unless a sailor wrote about the experience, the story of the voyage was lost. It was only when disaster struck and a ship went down that the details were deposited beneath the waves or noted in a document. Underwater archaeologists piece together the remains of shipwrecks and existing records to tell these stories today.

One of a Kind

Shipwrecks are like time capsules. They contain examples of what a culture made, ate, wore, traded, worked with, believed in, and discarded. They reveal details about the unique floating community that existed on a ship. And they provide evidence about the seafaring technology of past eras. Like our modern space-age science, seafaring often reflected the most advanced knowledge of the day.

Archaeological sites on land often have layers of remains from different groups who occupied the same place over time. But a shipwreck represents a single event in history. In most cases, everything on the site came from that particular ship.

Reasons for Wrecks

Modern mariners have many tools. Radios warn them of bad weather. Radar devices provide images of the shoreline and other ships nearby. Electronic instruments gather data from land and satellites to pinpoint a ship's location. Sailors of the past were at the mercy of nature and their own seafaring abilities. Their ships came to grief for many reasons.

Storms and hurricanes could surprise even the most experienced captain, and they often spelled disaster. Driving rain and waves could pound a ship until it capsized, broke apart, or

Ships often wrecked in stormy seas.

Shipboard Salvage

Sailors of the past removed hardware and equipment that could be used again before a rotten or damaged craft was left as a loss. When underwater archaeologists encounter a site that is missing certain common pieces, they consider the possibility that the ship did not wreck. Instead, they suspect that the vessel may have been salvaged before it was abandoned.

crashed on reefs, rocks, or shallow seabeds. As waves tossed a watercraft from side to side, burning lanterns or coals from the cookstove could ignite cargo or gunpowder, causing terror and tragedy. Even in calm weather, the danger of fire was a serious concern on a wooden ship.

Ships also ran aground because of errors in navigation. Early mariners relied on personal experience and information from other sailors to plan their course. Later, ships carried a compass and a few handheld instruments for determining direction and location. Sailors also had charts of coasts and harbors, but they were often inaccurate. Many vessels wrecked because the captain thought his ship was in safe water or because rocks and shallow areas were not marked on a chart.

Some vessels went to the bottom after encounters with enemies or pirates. In full-scale warfare, captains tried to destroy their opponent's ship. In minor fights, they preferred to disable the other vessel so it could be captured and sailed again by the victor. More than one crew intentionally **scuttled**, or sank, its vessel to keep it from being captured or to block a waterway so the enemy could not advance.

Sometimes ships just wore out, much as automobiles do today. As a vessel got old, its seams loosened up. Water seeped in through the planks, and no amount of bailing or pumping could keep it afloat. In warm water, a wood-eating marine worm, called a shipworm, bored into the hulls of ships, leaving them leaky and beyond repair.

Shipworms boring through wood can do extensive damage to a ship's hull.

Survival on the Seabed

Although books and television programs often leave the impression that ships sink only in warm, clear water, this is not true. The remains of watercraft are found in all types of water—fresh and salty, warm and cold, clear and dark. Some

Underwater wreckage of the famous luxury liner Titanic

are buried in beaches, and others lie hundreds of feet below the water. One of the most famous shipwrecks of all time, the *Titanic*, is 2.5 miles (4 kilometers) below the surface!

Several factors determine how well shipwreck remains have survived over time. One factor is the cause of the sinking. If a ship capsized, was scuttled, or had a small but fatal hole in the hull, it often landed on the bottom fairly intact. But if a ship crashed violently on rocks or a reef, it broke apart. The vessel and its contents were spread over a wide area. The crew sometimes added to the trail of destruction before the disaster. If they believed they were about to wreck, sailors tossed cannons, anchors, and cargo over the side to lighten the ship and reduce the chances of running aground.

The environment in which a wreck settled also affected its **preservation**. Water contains oxygen, which supports the growth of organisms that feed on natural materials such as wood, rope, and food. Oxygen also contributes to the decay, or corrosion, of metal objects. (The same process causes rust to form on metal items on land.) Metal artifacts corrode faster in warm water, where the oxygen content is high, and in salt water, which contains chemicals that speed the rate of decay.

Ships that sank in deep, cold freshwater are the best preserved. Less oxygen and fewer chemicals exist in this environment. In addition, wrecks in deep water are less affected by storms, currents, and waves. Combined with the chilly temperature, these conditions reduce the number of destructive organisms and slow the process of corrosion.

Vessels that settled in mud or loose sand also are well preserved. Portions of the lower hull and its contents often were buried quickly, protecting evidence of how the ship was built and what it carried. Over time, the exposed wooden parts rotted and collapsed. Hardware and artifacts from these upper

Divers use an underwater vacuum to clear a wreck of sand and other debris.

areas usually sank into the sediments or were covered by sand or coral on the seabed.

Nature was not very kind to ships that landed on rocks, a reef, or a hard bottom in shallow water. With little protection, they suffered the effects of waves, currents, storms, bacteria, and shipworms. Sites in these environments are a challenge to study because they are widely scattered and poorly preserved. Sometimes all that exists is a pile of ballast and heavier artifacts such as anchors or cannons.

A Point of Balance

Regardless of how and where they came to rest, most shipwrecks eventually reach a point of balance, or equilibrium, with their environment. The process of deterioration slows down or virtually stops because the surviving parts are waterlogged and covered by sediments, coral, or corrosion. As long as they are not disturbed by humans or a monumental force of nature such as a hurricane or an earthquake, they will continue to survive for hundreds or thousands of years.

This state of equilibrium has important consequences when shipwrecks are studied by underwater archaeologists. When remains are moved from their stable positions, they are reexposed to oxygen, chemicals, and organisms in the water. More important, when they are brought to the surface, they are returned to an oxygen-rich atmosphere. Unless they are treated properly, artifacts will not survive. Most objects must

Archaeologists sometimes transport artifacts, such as these parts of a cannon, in water to preserve them.

be kept wet until they undergo conservation. In addition, if an underwater site is not reburied when a project is over, parts of the ship left exposed will begin the process of deterioration and corrosion again.

This sponge harvester discovered an ancient Greek shipwreck while diving for sponges.

Chapter Four

Secrets to Success

Here's an interesting fact about underwater archaeology. Of the thousands of wrecks discovered worldwide, most were *not* located by underwater archaeologists. Most have been encountered accidentally by sponge divers, fishers, scuba divers, and others who spend time on the water or underwater for work or recreation. Treasure hunters have also found wrecks in their unending quest for fabled riches.

Changing Trends

While most shipwreck sites are still found accidentally, the pattern of discovery has changed in recent years. Increasingly, underwater archaeologists who work for universities, national or local governments, or private companies are leading projects to find and study specific sites. In addition, the behavior and attitude of the public toward underwater resources has changed. Laws and policies have been established to protect submerged sites from looting or destruction. People have become more aware of the value of wrecks and concerned about their preservation. Although treasure hunters still exist, it is much harder for them to operate without criticism or to sell artifacts that they recover.

The First Look

When a shipwreck is found accidentally, its identity is usually unknown. The challenge for researchers is to determine its age, origin, and importance. To do this, underwater archaeologists conduct a survey of the site to gather evidence. Surveys vary in nature, but they always begin with a dive to familiarize team members with the area. Divers investigate the size of the wreck, the artifacts, and the surviving pieces of the hull. During later dives, they examine the remains more closely. They fan away sediments with their hands to look for objects below the surface. They record the site by measuring important features, making a map, shooting photographs and videotape, and writing notes on underwater slates. They also recover artifacts that appear to be good clues, and they sometimes dig a few holes to see what is buried. This process is called "testing the site."

Critical Elements

Artifacts on the seabed do not necessarily indicate a shipwreck. Ballast and evidence of the hull also must be present.

32

Researchers gather evidence until they have a clear idea about the nationality, date, size, and function of the ship. They may be able to use old documents to identify the vessel more precisely. A project leader then must decide whether the site deserves further study. She or he must compare the knowledge that will be gained with the time and cost involved in excavating a wreck and conserving the artifacts.

Author KC Smith (at left) photographs an underwater site.

Sleuthing Clues

Because underwater research is time consuming and costly, archaeologists pick their projects carefully. They select sites that will answer numerous questions about a particular era or type of ship. Sometimes they decide to search for a famous vessel that was important in local or national history. In this case, the process of discovery is reversed: the identity of the wreck is known, but its exact location is not.

What sources of information do researchers use? The most valuable details are found in written records from the past. Collections of public papers (and the buildings in which they are kept) are called archives. Archival sources contain a wealth of information because governments, businesses, religious organizations, and other institutions kept records of their official transactions. Archives often also include materials such as letters, diaries, and journals from private individuals and organizations.

In particular, underwater archaeologists search for records about maritime traffic, commerce, and insurance. These provide details about the coming and going of ships, cargoes and supplies, and claims made after vessels were lost. Naval records are important because many ships were sunk or captured during military engagements. Researchers also rely on letters between royal courts and sea captains whose voyages to explore and colonize were often sponsored by a king or queen.

Libraries and museums hold a rich supply of evidence in their collections. For centuries, people have written books

about how to build ships, how to sail and navigate, and how to outfit a vessel. These works help underwater archaeologists identify artifacts and understand the jumbled remains of a ship's hull. People also have written about voyages and shipwrecks that they survived. True accounts allow researchers to reconstruct the history of a ship and the experiences of the people onboard. From old charts and maps, archaeologists can figure out what a captain knew about the waters in which he was sailing. In old paintings, they find illustrations of artifacts that are similar to objects found on the seabed.

Researchers use old books and navigational charts to reconstruct a wreck's history.

Modern Voices

People who live in areas where wrecks are thought to exist are another source of evidence. Fishing folk, divers, and members of families involved in seafaring for a long time know the surrounding waters and can provide useful information. They also know the folklore about stranded vessels that were salvaged and cargoes that washed ashore. A shipwreck was an exciting and profitable event for a small coastal community, so it is not surprising that tales about it would become part of the local history.

Coastal communities and fishers around the world have provided archaeologists with valuable information about local shipwrecks.

The Next Step

Archaeological evidence from a shipwreck tells only half of the story. Documents and people provide the rest of the story. Throughout a project, underwater archaeologists seek information in archives, libraries, and coastal communities to add to their understanding of the wreck and the history of the ship.

Suppose that you're an underwater archaeologist, and you've found a wreck that you want to study. You've done the background research. You've examined maps and charts and know generally where the site should be located. How do you find it?

Underwater archaeologists in this situation begin to search below the surface using two methods: remote sensing and visual exploration. Remote sensing requires specialized technical equipment. Visual exploration involves the use of divers. In either case, the bottom is scanned for anything that resembles cultural remains.

This diver relies on his scuba gear, a small pick, his underwater light, some rope, and a pouch to help him investigate a site.

Chapter Five

Tools of the Trade

Underwater archaeologists use many types of equipment to find, survey, record, and excavate sites. Their primary tool is scuba gear, which allows them to stay underwater for long periods of time. A basic diving kit includes a mask and fins, a tank of pressurized air, a regulator that turns high-pressure air in the tank into breathable air in a mouthpiece, a weight belt to keep a diver down, an inflatable vest, and a protective diving suit. Other items that improve the safety of a

An Important Invention

Jacques Cousteau and Emile Gagnon invented *scuba* in the 1940s. The term is an acronym for self-contained underwater breathing apparatus.

Researchers use a variety of electronic tools to locate wrecks on or under the seabed.

dive are a knife, a compass, and gauges to measure depth and the amount of air in the tank.

Because each site is different, underwater archaeologists adjust their equipment according to the conditions. They wear extra weight in the ocean because salt water is harder to sink in than freshwater. When the water is really cold, they wear special suits from head to toe to keep them dry and warm. When the water is so dark that they can't see 3 feet (0.9 m) in front of them, they use underwater lights and rely on their sense of touch.

Sometimes a wreck can be reached by swimming from shore, but researchers usually need a boat to get to their site. When a team is working far offshore, their boat is equipped

with a radio and electronic instruments that enable the captain to navigate, pinpoint the boat's location, and find the site. During an excavation, archaeologists often anchor a vessel, such as a barge, permanently over the wreck. This makes diving operations easier, and much of the equipment can be stored on the barge at night.

Views from Above

When underwater archaeologists are searching for a site, they use electronic or optical remote-sensing devices. These instruments allow them to scan large areas quickly. They also produce recorded images or responses that indicate the presence of deposits on or under the bottom. There are several different kinds of remote-sensing tools.

One set of remote-sensing tools measures changes in the earth's magnetic field. The most common is the **magnetometer**, or "mag." Most wrecks contain ferrous, or iron, artifacts such as anchors, cannons, and hardware. These objects on the

High in the Sky

The oldest remote-sensing technique—aerial photography—has been used by land archaeologists since the 1920s and by shipwreck archaeologists since the 1970s. At first, photos were taken from towers, balloons, and kites. Now, they are shot from airplanes. More recently, images from satellites have provided information about the contours and conditions of submerged areas. Eventually they may help to identify offshore sites.

Using a magnetometer

bottom create a variation in the local magnetic field. When an electronic sensor called a "fish" is towed over a concentration of iron, it sends a message to a unit on the boat. While mags can locate objects that are buried, they cannot identify materials made of other types of metal.

To find items that don't contain iron, underwater archaeologists use a metal detector. Divers with handheld units swim over a site to detect buried artifacts and determine the extent of the wreck.

Remote sensing also is conducted with sonar instruments—tools that locate objects by means of sound waves. The most common is the **fathometer**. This instrument determines water depth by measuring how long it takes for sound impulses to travel from the boat to the bottom and back. A sudden change in depth may indicate a site, although fathometers do not distinguish between wrecks, reefs, or rocks—a diver has to check to be sure.

Another sonar instrument is a side-scan sonar device. A "fish" towed behind the boat sends out sonar signals that strike the bottom and bounce back, or echo. The echoes reveal changes in the bottom contour. These are recorded on a printout or a digital display that can be downloaded on a computer. Used to find deepwater wrecks, side-scan sonar devices can detect non-iron materials, but they can't detect anything that is buried.

A third sonar instrument, the sub-bottom profiler, can find objects below the bottom. It transmits signals that penetrate seabed sediments until they hit bedrock and bounce back. Anything in the way returns the signals more quickly, and the response is recorded on a printed image.

Researchers prepare to lower a side-scan sonar device into the water to search for a wreck.

Sightings from Satellites

There is a joke about two fishermen who anchored on a reef one day and reeled in fish after fish. When it was time to leave, one man asked, "How will we find this place again?" The other man said, "Let's paint an X on the side of the boat!"

Underwater archaeolo-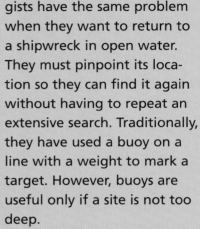gists have the same problem when they want to return to a shipwreck in open water. They must pinpoint its location so they can find it again without having to repeat an extensive search. Traditionally, they have used a buoy on a line with a weight to mark a target. However, buoys are useful only if a site is not too deep.

Increasingly, researchers are relying on GPS, or global positioning system (left), to record site locations. A small, handheld unit locks onto radio signals that are transmitted constantly from satellites in orbit. The device calculates the angles and distances of the signals and translates them into coordinates that represent an exact location. The coordinates are recorded in the unit's memory, and a team member also records them on paper. To return to that location, the coordinates are reentered into the device, which emits a beep when the position is reached.

Archaeologists also have used underwater vehicles called submersibles to locate and study shipwrecks. Towed or free-swimming, they are equipped with cameras and videos that allow team members to see what is on the bottom. The first manned submersible designed for underwater archaeology was built in 1964. About the same time, remotely operated vehicles, or ROVs, were developed. Since the mid-1980s,

Underwater vehicles called submersibles carry passengers.

ROVs have documented many ancient and modern wrecks in very deep water, including the *Titanic*.

Regardless of the devices they employ, researchers use controlled methods to search for a site. These materials ensure that they don't miss or repeat an area. The survey boat slowly travels back and forth in parallel lines, using electronic gear onboard or onshore to stay on course. One team member monitors the remote sensing receiver. When a likely target is recorded, another team member throws a weighted buoy or takes a GPS reading to mark the spot. Later, divers return to inspect the source of the unusual reading.

On-the-Spot Inspection

In clear shallow water, researchers can look for sites visually. Early wreck hunters used glass-bottomed boats or a water glass, a box with a clear window that allowed them to see below. Today, it is more common for swimmers with snorkeling gear to search by being pulled slowly behind a boat and holding on to a tow board.

Finding a shipwreck is one of the most challenging aspects of underwater archaeology. It requires research, equipment, logic, and patience. It can take days, months, and even years to find a site, and once it is located, the work has just begun.

Opposite: Glass-bottomed boats enable non-diving members of the public to view shipwrecks.

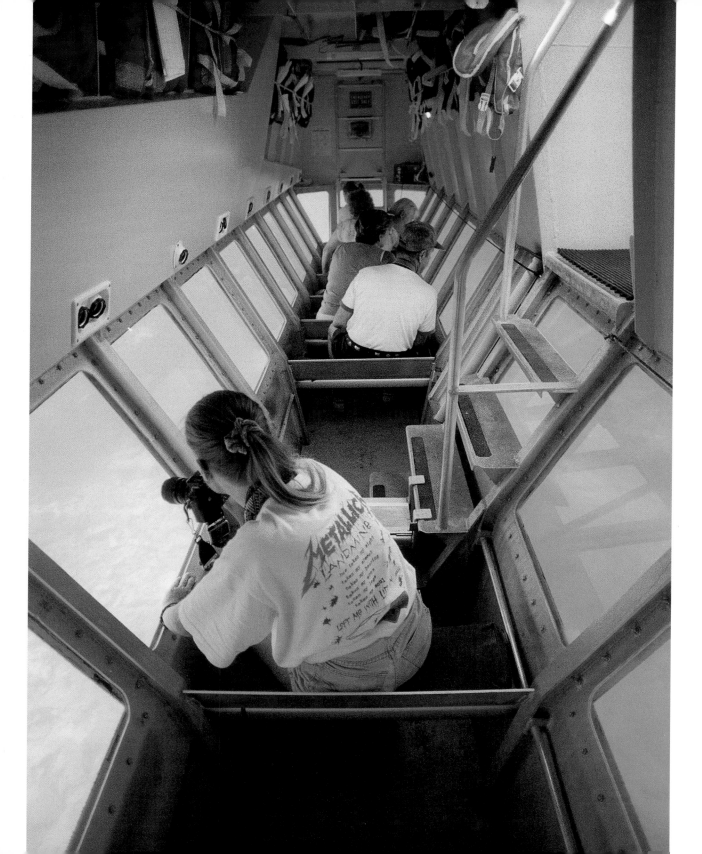

Experienced divers look for unnatural shapes underwater, such as these two cannons encrusted in sediments.

Chapter Six

More Than a Pile of Rocks

Some shipwrecks are hard to miss. Modern steel vessels, for example, are often so intact you can swim inside them. Other sites require a trained eye to spot. This is true of wooden wrecks, which often are scattered, decayed, and camouflaged. Underwater archaeologists look for shapes and mounds on the bottom that are different or unnatural.

Ballast piles are easy to spot because the rocks or chunks of iron carried in a ship's lower hull usually settled in one big

Evidence for the Future

The technology for recording and recovering minute details of a shipwreck has advanced amazingly in the past thirty years. Underwater archaeologists believe that it will continue to improve. Because of this, it is now common for researchers to excavate only part of a site. They gather as much evidence as they need to answer their research questions but leave the rest of the site intact for future investigation when more sophisticated recovery tools are available.

mass. Even when covered with coral, cannons and anchors are noticeable because they are large and have long and straight lines. Iron artifacts such as fasteners, hardware, or **rigging** for the sails stand out because **encrustation**—a coat of corrosion and sediments—gives them an odd appearance. Small, light artifacts are the hardest to see because they often have drifted into holes or settled into the bottom. Remains of the hull, the largest and most important artifact, may exist on the surface, but they are usually buried.

Finding a site is just the first step in the research process. The wreck must be identified, which requires work in the field, lab, and library. During fieldwork, underwater archaeologists conduct a survey or an excavation. A survey involves limited testing and the recovery of a sample of diagnostic artifacts. During an excavation, researchers examine and recover most of the remains. Occasionally, they bring up the pieces of the hull so the ship can be reconstructed and displayed in a museum. But this is a costly and time-consuming venture. In most cases, researchers leave the pieces on the bottom after they record their observations and create a picture of the hull with drawings, photos, and videotape.

The Real Archaeology

Anything left on the bottom must be reburied, and anything brought to the surface must be conserved. In fact, most of the archaeology takes place in the laboratory, where artifacts are cleaned, stabilized, recorded, and analyzed. As mud and encrustation are removed, objects turn into wonderful discoveries. To understand these new puzzle pieces, team members consult books, documents, and other experts, and they compare their evidence to similar archaeological sites elsewhere. In the end, underwater archaeologists try to create a whole and accurate picture of the ill-fated vessel and the culture that built and used it.

After artifacts have been cleaned and recorded, archaeologists begin to analyze the information.

There is more to a project than just putting the puzzle together. Underwater archaeologists must share their findings. While they are studying a site, they give lectures to inform others about their progress. At the end of the research, team members prepare a comprehensive report about the discovery of the wreck, the artifacts and evidence that were recovered, the historical details about the ship, and the meaning and significance of the site. They share their findings with the public through lectures, newspaper and magazine articles, books, and documentaries. They help museums to create exhibits that display artifacts and information. Most important, underwater archaeologists tell students of all ages about their work so future generations will understand and appreciate the past.

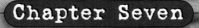

Chapter Seven

Exploring On Your Own

You are never too young to learn about underwater archaeology and become involved in the preservation of cultural sites. Books and magazine articles are available for kids who want to know about shipwrecks and how they are explored. The World Wide Web has lots of information about underwater archaeology and maritime history, from research reports and bibliographies to lists of museums that you can visit and universities where you can train.

Local colleges and societies sponsor lectures that you can attend. Or you can invite an underwater archaeologist to your class to give a talk. Museums that feature maritime exhibits often present special programs during the school year and camps in the summer that focus on underwater archaeology. In addition, educational materials are available for the classroom, so you might ask your teacher to present several lessons about a specific project or the profession. Finally, shipwrecks and artifact conservation provide interesting topics for history or science fair projects.

The most important way that you can be involved is to consider the value of shipwreck sites. Very few wrecks contain treasure in the form of gold, silver, and jewels. However, they all contain a treasure trove of information about the past. Underwater sites belong to the public. We are stewards responsible for their protection. The way that people preserve shipwrecks today will affect our ability to learn from them tomorrow.

Opposite: Kids interested in underwater archaeology can take part in special maritime programs at school or summer camp.

Glossary

archaeologists—scientists who study past cultures based on artifacts and other evidence left behind

artifacts—objects made or modified by humans

ballast—heavy material such as rocks or pieces of iron placed in the lower part of a ship for stability

conservation; conservator—the documentation, analysis, cleaning, and treatment of an object to ensure its survival; one who is responsible for conservation

cultures—the institutions, tools, customs, rituals, and beliefs of a group of people

encrustation—a coat of corrosion and sediments that forms on metal objects in seawater

excavation—the scientific recovery of the remains of past human activity

fathometer—a sonar instrument that determines water depth by measuring sound impulses

hull—the body of a ship

hypothesis—an unproved idea that is accepted for purposes of argument or further study

magnetometer—a remote-sensing tool that measures changes in the earth's magnetic field

maritime archaeologists—scientists who examine ships, people, and societies involved in seafaring

nautical archaeologists—scientists who study how and why vessels were built, what kind of equipment and skills were needed to operate them, and what routes were traveled

prehistoric underwater archaeologists—scientists who study human activity that occurred around water before written records

preservation—the extent to which something has survived over time

rigging—the ropes, chains, and other gear used to support, position, and control masts and sails on a ship

scientific method—the systematic testing of a hypothesis

scuttle—to sink a ship by cutting holes through the bottom or sides

sediments—sand or stones deposited by water, wind, or glaciers

treasure hunters—untrained divers who dig up underwater sites for financial gain

To Find Out More

Books

Ballard, Robert D. *Exploring the Titanic.* Toronto: Scholastic/ Madison Press Books, 1988.

Blackman, Steve. *Ships and Shipwrecks.* New York: Franklin Watts, 1993.

Humble, Richard. *Submarines and Ships.* New York: Viking/ Penguin Putnam, 1997.

Lerner Geography Department. *Sunk! Exploring Underwater Archaeology.* Minneapolis: Runestone Press, 1994.

Macaulay, David. *Ship.* Boston: Houghton Mifflin Company, 1993.

Platt, Richard. *Shipwreck*. New York: Alfred A. Knopf, 1997.

Schultz, Ron, Nick Gadbois, and Peter Aschwanden. *Looking Inside Sunken Treasure*. Santa Fe: John Muir Publications, 1993.

Tritton, Roger, ed. *The Visual Dictionary of Ships and Sailing*. New York: Dorling Kindersley, 1991.

On-the-Spot Inspection

Archaeological Institute of America
656 Beacon Street
Boston, MA 02215–2010
http://www.archaeological.org/
This website offers up-to-date information about the archaeology profession.

British Sub-Aqua Club
Telford's Quay
Ellesmere Port, South Wirral
Cheshire L65 4FY, England
http://www.bsac.com/
This website provides information about learning to dive.

Florida State University Directory of Underwater Archaeology
http://www.adp.fsu.edu/uwdirect.html
This website provides information about the university's current projects and other links.

How to Do Maritime Research on the Internet
Peter McCracken, editor
University of Washington Libraries
P.O. Box 353080
Seattle, WA 98195-3080
http://ils.unc.edu/maritime/home.html
This website provides general maritime information and several useful links.

Institute of Nautical Archaeology
P.O. Drawer HG
College Station, TX 77841–5137
http://nautarch.tamu.edu/ina/
This website provides information about the institute's projects.

Nordic Underwater Archaeology
Per Åkesson, editor
http://www.abc.se/~m10354/uwa/index.html
This website focuses on underwater sites in northern Europe.

A Note on Sources

Because I've worked on research projects to find historic wrecks, I've seen some of the techniques that underwater archaeologists use. When I wrote *Exploring for Shipwrecks*, these experiences and observations helped me to select the information that I wanted to share. I made an outline of the important details, and then I began to write.

When I needed to check facts, I consulted books in the library that my husband and I have acquired over the years. Much of the information I needed was available in my own home. When I had specific questions, I telephoned archaeologists to seek their knowledge and advice.

My experience in writing this book offers a good tip for kids. If you are interested in a topic, become involved in related activities and collect as many books as you can about the subject. Practical knowledge and a personal library are resources that you will rely on again and again.

—*KC Smith*

Index

Numbers in *italics* indicate illustrations.

aerial photography, 41
aircraft carriers, 21–22
archaeology, 8, 12–13, *12.*
    See also underwater
    archaeology.
    archival resources, 34–35,
    35, 37
    hypothesis, development
    of, 12
    maritime archaeology, 13
    nautical archaeology, 14
    prehistoric underwater
    archaeology, 13
    project selection, 34
    project teams, 15
    scientific method, 12
    site conservation, 18–19,
    26, 50, 53
    site documentation, *18–
    19*
artifacts, 7, 9, *17*, 27–28, 32,

48. See also treasure
    hunters.
ballast stones, 6
cataloging, *12*, *15*, 51
Cayman Islands project, 9
conservation, 14, *14*, 28,
    29, 50–51, *51*, 53
corrosion, 26–27, 29
identifying, *10*, 35, 49
olive jars, *8*, 9

ballast, 6, 32, 49–50

conservation, 28, *29*, 50–51,
    51, 53
    of archaeological sites,
    18–19, 26, 50, 53
    of artifacts, 14, *14*
    encrustation, 50
    point of balance, 28
coral reefs, 6

coralheads, 6
Cousteau, Jacques, 40

encrustation, 50

fathometer, 42–43
fish (electronic sensor),
    42–43

Gagnon, Emile, 40
glass-bottomed boats, 46, *47*
global positioning system
    (GPS), 44, *44*

magnetometer, 41–42, *42*
maritime archaeology, 13
Mediterranean Sea, 31
metal detectors, 42

nautical archaeology, 14

paleontology, 12
point of balance, 28
prehistoric underwater
    archaeology, 13
preservation, 26, *29*
project selection, 34
project teams, 15

reefs, 6

remote-sensing tools, 37, *40*
    fish (electronic sensor),
        42–43
    magnetometer, 41–42, *42*
    sonar instruments, 42–43,
        46
remotely operated vehicles
    (ROVs), 45–46
ROVs. *See* remotely oper-
    ated vehicles.

schooners, *20–21*
scuba gear, 39–40
scuttled vessels, 24
shipworms, 25, *25*, 28
shipwrecks, 22, *23*
    aerial photography of, 41
    causes of, 22–25
    in deep water, 27
    partial excavation of, 50
    people as source of evi-
        dence of, 36
    point of balance, 28
    site conservation, 18–19,
        26, 50, 53
    "testing the site," 32
side-scan sonar, 43, *43*
site conservation, 18–19, 26,
    50, 53
Smith, KC, *33*

sonar instruments
 fathometers, 42–43
 remote sensing receivers,
  46
 side-scan sonar, 43
 sub-bottom profiler, 43
sponge harvesters, *30*, 31
sub-bottom profiler, 43
submersibles, 45, *45*
supertankers, 21–22

Titanic, 26, *26*, 46
treasure hunters, 16–17. *See
 also* artifacts.

underwater archaeology, *4*,
 5–9, *10*, 11, 16–18, *16*,
 17, 22, *27*, *33*, 49,
 52–53. *See also* archaeology.
 artifact identification, *10*,
  35, 49
 equipment, *38–39*, 39–41,
  40, *42*
 prehistoric underwater
  archaeology, 13
 remote-sensing tools, 37,
  40, 41
 project reports and lec-
  tures, 51

project selection, 34
project teams, 15
sponge harvesters and, *30*,
 31
"testing the site," 32
treasure hunters compared
 to, 16–17
visual exploration, 37
World Wide Web and, 52-
 53

vessels, 21
 aircraft carriers, 21–22
 as archaeological equip-
  ment, 40–41, 45–46, *47*
 ballast, 32, 49–50
 encrustation, 50
 equipment salvage, 24
 glass-bottomed boats, 46,
  47
 hull, 6
 remotely operated vehicles
  (ROVs), 45–46
 rigging, 50
 schooners, *20–21*
 scuttling, 24
 shipwrecks, 22–23
 submersibles, 45, *45*
 supertankers, 21–22
visual exploration, 37

About the Author

Since 1976, KC Smith has worked on underwater archaeological projects in the United States, the Caribbean, and Africa. As program supervisor at the Museum of Florida History in Tallahassee, she develops educational programs about history, archaeology, and folklife. KC Smith is a charter member of the Society for American Archaeology Public Education Committee and coedits its publication, *Teaching with Archaeology*. She has also edited the Institute of Nautical Archaeology newsletter.

KC Smith has studied humanities, archaeology, and history at Florida Atlantic University, Texas A & M University, and Florida State University. Her interest in shipwrecks comes from helping her husband Roger, an underwater archaeologist, with research projects. She believes that the findings from such projects should be shared with the public, especially young people. KC Smith is the author of the Watts Library books *Ancient Shipwrecks* and *Shipwrecks of the Explorers*.